Cookies
Quick and Easy

h.f.ullmann

Cookies – Quick and Easy
© 2009 Tandem Verlag GmbH
h.f.ullmann is an imprint of Tandem Verlag GmbH
All rights reserved

Original title: Plätzchenbacken schnell und leicht
ISBN: 978-3-8331-7042-3

Text: Gisela Muhr for agilmedien, Niederkassel
Cover design: Simone Sticker
Cover photography: © Tandem Verlag GmbH/TLC Fotostudio GmbH
Photography book: © Tandem Verlag GmbH/TLC Fotostudio GmbH
Photography flyer: © Tandem Verlag GmbH/TLC Fotostudio GmbH
Layout: Derek Gotzen/A. Aspropoulos for agilmedien, Niederkassel
Complete production: Tandem Verlag GmbH, Potsdam

© 2011 for the English edition: Tandem Verlag GmbH
h.f.ullmann is an imprint of Tandem Verlag GmbH

Overall responsibility for production: h.f.ullmann publishing, Potsdam, Germany

Translation into English: Tammi Reichel, APE Int'l, LLC
Typesetting and production: Sabine Brand, typeXpress, Köln

Printed and produced in China

ISBN 978-3-8331-6090-5

10 9 8 7 6 5 4 3 2 1
X IX VIII VII VI V IV III II I

www.ullmann-publishing.com
newsletter@ullmann-publishing.com

Contents

Introduction

Cookies as if by Magic

Preparations for Christmas typically begin at the end of November, and cookies are simply an indispensable element of a beautiful Advent and Christmas season. The aroma of cinnamon, cloves and other ingredients wafts through the house and heightens our anticipation of the coming holidays.

Homemade cookies taste the best, and with this practical cookie cutter nothing could be easier. With a flick of the wrist, you can cut thirty-four cookies of various shapes out of your rolled-out dough! This economy saves valuable minutes, helping ensure that the days leading up to the holidays aren't frantic, but a time for reflection and enjoyment.

The forty recipes in this collection include something for everyone. The Christmas treats in the first section are as easy as pie to cut out with our cookie cutter. Just press it firmly into the dough, and move the cookie cutter gently back and forth. The second section contains recipes for additional classic cookies that should not be missing from your repertoire, at the holidays and year round.

Bake often! You'll soon find that ease of preparation and fantastic baked treats are not mutually exclusive!

Storing Cookies

Cookies keep best if they are layered and stored in cookie tins. Always place wax paper or parchment paper between the layers so that the cookies lie flat and are less likely to break. The aromas of richly spiced cookies including cinnamon, cloves, etc. can permeate the entire tin, so it's best to avoid mixing them with other types of cookies. Be sure to allow cookies with chocolate glaze and other frosted or iced items to dry completely before storing them. Cookies will stay fresh for up to four weeks in a well-sealed tin.

Gingerbread cookies are very firm when they come out of the oven and should be left uncovered, at room temperature, for one or two days. As they absorb humidity from the air, they become softer again. Gingerbread cookies should also be stored in tins. They will stay soft and moist for longer if you add a few apple slices to the tin.

Making Cookie Dough

You can certainly make short pastry with a hand mixer, but this type of dough will turn out even better if it is kneaded by hand. Sift the flour onto a clean work surface, form a hollow in the middle and pour the egg or eggs into the hollow. Place the butter, cut into small pieces, around the rim of the flour, then add the remaining ingredients. Quickly knead all of it into a smooth dough with your hands. Form the dough into a ball, cover it with plastic wrap and let it rest in the fridge. How long you rest the dough depends on the particular recipe. Firmly knead the dough again by hand before going on to the next step.

If you'd like to make more than thirty-four cookies, simply double the recipe.
The sky is the limit as far as glazes and icings for the recipes on the following pages are concerned. You can decorate them any way you like – or not at all.

Have fun baking with your new cookie cutter!

Cookie Cut

ter Recipes

Buttermilk cookies

2 ¾ cups/370 g flour
1 cup + 2 tbsp/250 g butter
6 tbsp buttermilk
2 egg yolks
⅔ cup/150 g decorating sugar

Mix together the flour, butter and buttermilk by hand and knead them into a dough. Cover the dough and let it rest in the fridge for 1 hour.
Preheat the oven to 350°F/175°C. Roll out the dough on a floured work surface to a thickness of about 5 cm/⅕ inch. Use the cookie cutter to cut out the cookies and place them on a baking sheet lined with parchment paper. Whisk the egg yolks with 2 tbsp water. Spread the egg yolk on the cookies and sprinkle with the decorating sugar.
Bake the cookies for approximately 10 minutes.

Preparation time: 20 minutes (excluding resting time for the dough)

Egg liqueur cookies with chocolate

1 cup + 2 tbsp/250 g butter
⅓ cup/75 g sugar
½ cup/125 ml egg liqueur
(Advocaat, for example)
2 tbsp vinegar
3 cups/400 g flour

For the icing:
7 oz/200 g milk chocolate
6 tbsp egg liqueur

Beat the butter, sugar and egg liqueur until fluffy. Stir in the vinegar, then gradually add the flour and knead the mixture thoroughly by hand. Cover the dough with plastic wrap and let it rest in the fridge for several hours.

Preheat the oven to 390°F/200°C. On a floured work surface, roll out the dough evenly. Cut out the cookies and place them on baking sheets lined with parchment paper. Bake the cookies for approximately 8 minutes, or until golden brown.

For the icing, melt the chocolate in a water bath, then remove the pan from the stove and stir in the egg liqueur. Spread the chocolate mixture on the cookies with a wide-bladed knife. Place on a cooling rack to dry.

Preparation time: 40 minutes (excluding resting time for the dough)

Almond cookies

1 ½ cups/200 g flour
⅓ cup/75 g sugar
1 pinch salt
1 egg
1 egg white
seeds of ½ vanilla bean

generous 1 cup/100 g ground
almonds
7 tbsp/100 g butter
1 egg yolk
scant ½ cup/50 g slivered
almonds

Sift the flour onto a clean work surface. Form a hollow in the middle and place the sugar, salt, egg, egg white, vanilla seeds and ground almonds in it. Cut the butter into little pieces and place them around the rim of the flour. Using your hands, knead everything together into a smooth dough. Cover the dough in plastic wrap and let it rest in the fridge for 1 hour.
Preheat the oven to 320°F/160°C. Roll out the dough on a floured work surface, cut out the cookies, and place them on a baking sheet lined with parchment paper. Whisk the egg yolk with 1 tbsp water. Brush the egg yolk onto the cookies and sprinkle with the slivered almonds.
Bake the cookies for approximately 10–12 minutes.

Preparation time: 20 minutes (excluding resting time for the dough)

Sweet pastry cookies

2 ¼ cups/300 g flour
⅔ cup/150 g sugar
2 egg yolks
14 tbsp/200 g chilled butter
2 tbsp cream

For the glaze:
1 cup + 2 tbsp/125 g
confectioners' sugar
2–3 tbsp raspberry syrup
decorating sugar

Quickly knead together the flour, sugar, egg yolks, butter and cream into a crumbly dough. Cover the dough in plastic wrap and let it rest in the fridge for 1 hour.
Preheat the oven to 355°F/180°C and cover a baking sheet with parchment paper. Sprinkle flour on a clean work surface. Roll out the dough to a thickness of ⅓ inch/1 cm and cut out the cookies. Lay them on the baking sheet and bake for approximately 12 minutes, or until golden brown. Transfer to a rack to cool. For the glaze, combine the confectioners' sugar and raspberry syrup, stir well and brush over the cookies. Then sprinkle with decorating sugar and allow to dry.

Preparation time: 30 minutes (excluding resting time for the dough)

Czech cookies

1 cup + 2 tbsp/250 g butter
3 egg yolks
3 tbsp sugar
2 cups/275 g flour

1 egg white

1 cup + 2 tbsp/125 g
confectioners' sugar, sifted
2 tsp vanilla sugar, or ¼ tsp
vanilla extract
2 tbsp slivered almonds
1 tbsp small raisins or currants

Thoroughly mix the butter, egg yolks and sugar, then knead in
the flour. Form the dough into a ball and cover it with plastic
wrap. Let the dough rest in the fridge for 1 hour.
Preheat the oven to 320°F/160°C. Roll out the dough thinly on
a floured work surface. Cut out the cookies and place them on
a baking sheet lined with parchment paper. For the topping,
place the egg white in a bowl and whisk with the confectioners'
sugar and vanilla sugar or extract. Spread the mixture onto the
cookies and then sprinkle with sliced almonds and raisins or
currants.
Bake for approximately 10 minutes.

Preparation time: 20 minutes (excluding resting time for the dough)

Amaretto cookies

4 eggs
9 tbsp/125 g sugar
1 cup + 2 tbsp/250 g butter
3 ½ cups/500 g flour
8 tbsp almond liqueur
(Amaretto)

scant 1 cup/100 g confectioners'
sugar

Hard-boil three of the eggs. Combine the cooked egg yolks (the
egg whites are not needed) with the additional raw egg, sugar,
butter, flour and 6 tbsp almond liqueur and knead into a smooth
dough. Form the dough into a ball, cover it in plastic wrap and
let it rest in the fridge for 2 hours.
Preheat the oven to 340°F/170°C. Roll out the dough thinly on
a floured work surface. Cut out the cookies, bake on a tray for
approximately 10 minutes, then let them cool thoroughly.
Make a glaze from the remaining almond liqueur and the
confectioners' sugar and brush it over the cookies.

Preparation time: 30 minutes (excluding resting time for the dough)

Gingerbread with candied fruit (Lebkuchen)

¾ cup/250 g honey
1 cup + 2 tbsp/250 g cane sugar
⅔ cup/150 g butter
1 egg
generous 1 cup/
100 g ground almonds
3 cups/400 g flour
1 tbsp cocoa powder
1 tsp ground cinnamon
2 tsp pumpkin pie spice
1 tbsp lemon zest
1 tbsp potash (or baking soda)
2 tbsp rum

For the icing:
1 ⅓ cups/
150 g confectioners' sugar
3 tbsp lemon juice
3–4 oz/100 g chopped candied fruits
3–4 oz/100 g candied cherries

Heat the honey, cane sugar and butter in a saucepan, stirring continuously until the sugar melts. Pour into a wide mixing bowl and let cool. Add the egg, ground almonds, flour, cocoa powder, spices, and lemon zest and knead thoroughly with the dough hook of an electric mixer. Thoroughly blend the potash (or baking soda) with the rum. Add to the dough and continue kneading until the dough is glossy and no longer sticky. You may need to add more flour. Cover the bowl with plastic wrap and refrigerate overnight.

Preheat the oven to 355 °F/180 °C. Divide the dough into two portions and roll out one at a time on a lightly floured work surface. Cut out the cookies. Place them on a baking sheet dusted with flour and bake for approximately 18 minutes. Remove the cookies from the baking sheet carefully, as they will be very soft. Place on rack to cool.

For the icing, stir the powdered sugar and lemon juice into a smooth mixture and brush it on the cookies. The icing hardens very quickly, so be sure to top them with the candied fruits and cherries right away. Allow to dry thoroughly and store in an airtight tin.

Preparation time: 45 minutes (excluding resting time for the dough)

Puff pastry cookies

1 package frozen puff pastry
(9 oz/250 g)
1 egg yolk
1 tbsp milk
4 tbsp apricot jam
2 tbsp lemon juice

1 tbsp ground almonds
2 tbsp decorating sugar

Let the puff pastry thaw. Preheat the oven to 355 °F/180 °C. Roll out the puff pastry on a floured
work surface. Cut out the cookies and place them on a baking sheet lined with parchment paper.
Combine the egg yolk and milk, mix well, and brush the cookies with the mixture.
Bake the cookies for approximately 15 minutes or until golden brown. In the meantime, warm the
apricot jam, combine it with the lemon juice and ground almonds, and spread it on the cookies while
they are still warm. For the finishing touch, sprinkle them with decorating sugar.

Preparation time: 40 minutes (excluding resting time for the dough)

Marzipan-nougat cookies

2 cups/275 g flour
⅔ cup/150 g sugar
2 tsp vanilla sugar,
or ¼ tsp vanilla extract
2 egg yolks
¾ cup/175 g chilled butter

14 oz/400 g marzipan paste
2–3 egg whites
9 oz/250 g nougat

Sift the flour onto a clean work surface and form a hollow in the middle of the mound. Place the sugar, vanilla sugar (or extract) and egg yolks in the hollow. Cut the butter into small pieces and place them on the outer edges of the flour. With your hands, quickly work all the ingredients into a smooth dough. Form the dough into a ball. Cover with plastic wrap and let it rest in the fridge for 2 hours.

Preheat the oven to 355 °F/180 °C. Roll out the dough on a floured work surface. Cut out the cookies and place them on a baking sheet lined with parchment paper.

Make a smooth mixture out of the marzipan, egg whites and a little water. Fill a pastry bag with the mixture and pipe a border around the top of the cookies. Bake for approximately 10 minutes. Melt the nougat in a double boiler and, using a teaspoon, fill the middle of each marzipan "wreath" with it. Allow the nougat mixture to solidify before eating the cookies.

Preparation time: 50 minutes (excluding resting time for the dough)

Chocolate walnut cookies

1 ¾ cups/250 g flour
½ tsp baking powder
9 tbsp/125 g sugar
1 egg
9 tbsp/125 g butter, softened
2 tbsp milk
⅔ cup/60 g ground walnuts

⅔ cup/60 g ground almonds
½ cup/60 g raisins, chopped
3–4 oz/100 g semisweet
chocolate, grated
scant 1 cup/100 g confectioners'
sugar
1 ⅓ cups/150 g walnut halves

Combine the flour and baking powder and sift into a mixing bowl. Add the sugar, egg, butter and milk and mix well. Thoroughly knead it, using the dough hook of an electric mixer. Work in the ground walnuts and almonds, raisins and grated chocolate. Knead the dough well by hand, shape it into a ball, cover with plastic wrap and let it rest in the refrigerator for 2 hours.
Preheat the oven to 355 °F/180 °C. Roll out the dough on a floured work surface and cut out the cookies. Place them on a baking sheet lined with parchment paper and bake for 8 to 10 minutes. Stir the confectioners' sugar with 2 teaspoons water until smooth. Place a dab on each cookie and top with a walnut half.

Preparation time: 40 minutes (excluding resting time for the dough)

Jelly-filled hazelnut cookies

3 cups/400 g flour
1 ¾ cups/
200 g confectioners' sugar
1 ⅔ cups/125 g ground
hazelnuts
9 tbsp/125 g chilled butter

1 egg
1 egg yolk
4 tbsp blackberry jelly

Combine the flour, 1 ¾ cups/200 g of the confectioners' sugar and the ground hazelnuts and sift onto a work surface. Form a hollow in the middle of the mound. Cut the butter into small pieces and place along the rim of the flour mixture. Place the egg and egg yolk in the hollow. Using your hands, quickly knead all the ingredients into a smooth dough. Shape it into a ball, cover with plastic wrap and let it rest in the fridge for 2 hours.

Preheat the oven to 300°F/150°C. Roll out the dough on a floured work surface. Cut out the cookies, place them on a baking sheet lined with parchment paper, and bake for approximately 10 minutes.

In a small bowl, stir the blackberry jelly until smooth. Briefly cool the baked cookies.

Place a dab of blackberry jelly on half of the cookies, then firmly top these with another one.

Preparation time: 30 minutes (excluding resting time for the dough)

Dutch Christmas cookies

1 ½ cups/200 g flour	9 tbsp/125 g butter
9 tbsp/75 g cornstarch	1 ⅓ cups/150 g confectioners' sugar
⅓ cup/75 g sugar	14 oz/400 g marzipan paste
1 pinch salt	⅓ cup/100 g orange marmalade
2 tsp vanilla sugar or	4–5 oz/125 g bittersweet
¼ tsp vanilla extract	chocolate (coating chocolate,
1 egg	if available)

Blend the flour, cornstarch, sugar, salt and vanilla sugar (if using extract, add with the egg) in a bowl. Add the egg and butter cut into small pieces and knead by hand into a smooth dough. Cover in plastic wrap and let it rest in the fridge for at least 1 hour. Meanwhile, knead two-thirds of the confectioners' sugar into the marzipan. Sprinkle the rest of the confectioners' sugar over the work surface and roll out the marzipan very thinly. Use the cookie cutter to cut out shapes and set aside. Preheat the oven to 350°F/175°C. Roll out the dough on a floured surface to a thickness of ca. ⅛ inch/3 mm. Cut out the cookies and place them on a baking sheet lined with parchment paper. Bake for about 10 minutes and let cool thoroughly. Heat the orange marmalade in a small saucepan or microwave and brush it on the cookies. Place a marzipan shape on top of each cookie and press down lightly. Coarsely chop the bittersweet chocolate and melt it in a double boiler. Coat half of each cookie and allow to set before eating.

Preparation time: 50 minutes (excluding resting time for the dough)

Spekulatius

2 ½ tsp baking powder	2 tsp vanilla sugar or ¼ tsp vanilla
3 ¾ cups/500 g flour	extract
1 cup + 2 tbsp/250 g sugar	1 tsp cinnamon
2 eggs	¼ tsp each, ground cloves and
1 cup + 2 tbsp/250 g chilled butter	cardamom
100 g ground almonds	¼ tsp ground nutmeg
¼ cup/50 g demerara sugar	⅛ tsp ground coriander

Sift the flour and baking powder onto a work surface and form a hollow in the middle of the mound. Add the sugar and eggs to the hollow. Cut the butter into small pieces and place along the rim of the flour mixture. Use your hands to work everything into a smooth dough, adding all the remaining ingredients in the process. Form the dough into a ball, cover in plastic wrap and let it rest in the fridge for 2 hours.
Preheat the oven to 300 °F/150 °C. On a floured work surface, roll out the dough evenly, cut out the cookies and place on a baking sheet lined with parchment paper. Bake for approximately 15 minutes or until golden brown.

Preparation time: 35 minutes (excluding resting time for the dough)

Sesame seed cookies

1 ⅔ cups/375 g butter
¾ cup + 2 tbsp/200 g sugar
5 egg yolks
3 ¾ cups/500 g flour
7 tbsp/50 g confectioners' sugar
⅔ cup/100 g sesame seeds

Beat the butter until light and fluffy. Beat in the sugar and egg yolks and mix well. Add the flour gradually, working it in by hand and kneading into a smooth dough. Form the dough into a ball, cover with plastic wrap and let it rest in the fridge for 2 hours. Preheat the oven to 355 °F/180 °C. On a floured work surface, roll out the dough thinly. Cut out the cookies, place them on a baking sheet lined with parchment paper and bake for 10 to 12 minutes.
Make a glaze of the confectioners' sugar and 1 teaspoon water. Brush it on the cookies and roll them in the sesame seeds.

Preparation time: 35 minutes (excluding resting time for the dough)

Butter cookies

1 ¾ cups/250 g flour
1 cup + 2 tbsp/125 g
confectioners' sugar
grated peel of ½ lemon
1 egg
⅔ cup/150 g chilled butter

For the glaze:
1 cup + 2 tbsp/125 g
confectioners' sugar
2–3 tbsp lemon juice
sugar pearls to decorate

Combine the flour, confectioners' sugar and lemon zest and mound it on a work surface. Make a well in the middle and crack the egg into it. Distribute the butter, cut in small pieces, around the edge. Chop through everything with a knife, then knead by hand into a firm dough. Shape it into a ball, cover with plastic wrap and let the dough rest in the fridge for at least 1 hour.
Preheat the oven to 355 °F/180 °C. On a floured surface, roll out the dough to a thickness of ca. ⅛ inch/3 mm. Cut out the cookies, place them on a baking sheet and bake for approximately 10 minutes or until golden brown. Place the cookies on a rack and let them cool thoroughly.
For the glaze, blend the confectioners' sugar and lemon juice until smooth. Lightly coat the cookies with it and decorate with sugar pearls according to taste.

Preparation time: 45 minutes (excluding resting time for the dough)

Candied fruit cookies

2 ¼ cups/300 g flour
7 tbsp/100 g sugar
1 pinch salt
2 tsp vanilla sugar or
¼ tsp vanilla extract
1 egg

14 tbsp/200 g chilled butter
1 tbsp candied cherries
1 tbsp candied orange peel
1 tbsp candied lemon peel
1 egg yolk
2 tbsp chopped brittle

Sift the flour and combine with the sugar, salt and vanilla sugar (if using extract, add with the egg). Mound this on a work surface. Make a hollow in the middle and put the egg in it. Spread the butter, cut into small pieces, around the edge. Knead everything by hand into a smooth dough. Finely chop the candied cherries, orange peel and lemon peel and stir into the dough. Cover it in plastic wrap and let it rest in the fridge for 1 hour. Line the baking sheet with parchment paper and preheat the oven to 320 °F/160 °C. Dust the work surface with flour, roll out the dough to a thickness of ca. ⅕ inch/5 mm and cut out the cookies. Place them on the baking sheet and brush each cookie with the egg yolk whisked with 1–2 teaspoons water. Sprinkle the brittle on the cookies and bake for 12 to 15 minutes or until golden brown.

Preparation time: 25 minutes (excluding resting time for the dough)

Quince-filled sweet pastry biscuits

1 ¾ cups/250 g flour
1 ½ tsp baking powder
7 tbsp/100 g sugar
generous ½ cup/50 g ground
almonds
¼ tsp ground cardamom

¼ tsp ground cloves
½ tsp cinnamon
1 egg
9 tbsp/125 g chilled butter
⅓ cup/100 g quince jelly
confectioners' sugar

Thoroughly combine the flour, baking powder, sugar, ground almonds and spices. Add the egg and the butter cut into small pieces and quickly knead by hand into a smooth dough. Form the dough into a ball, cover it with plastic wrap and let it rest in the fridge for 30 minutes.
Preheat the oven to 350°F/175°C. On a floured work surface, roll out the dough thinly and cut out the cookies. Use a thimble or other small round object to cut the center out of half the cookies. Place all the cookies on a baking sheet lined with parchment paper and bake for approximately 10 minutes. Transfer to a rack to cool.
Warm the quince jelly. Spread jelly on each of the cookies without a hole. Top each of them with a cookie that has a hole in the center and sprinkle liberally with confectioners' sugar.

Preparation time: 25 minutes (excluding resting time for the dough)

Lemon-iced gingerbread cookies

2 ¼ cups/300 g flour
7 tbsp/100 g sugar
2 tsp pumpkin pie spice
1 ½ tsp baking powder
2 tbsp cocoa powder
1 egg

14 tbsp/200 g chilled butter

For the icing:
1 cup + 2 tbsp/125 g
confectioners' sugar
2–3 tbsp lemon juice

Sift the flour onto a work surface. Add the other dry ingredients, egg and butter cut into small pieces. Starting from the outside, knead everything together by hand to form a smooth dough. Form the dough into a ball, cover with plastic wrap and let it rest in the fridge for 2 hours.
Preheat oven to 355 °F/180 °C. On a work surface dusted with flour, roll out the dough to a thickness of ca. ⅓ inch/1 cm and cut out the cookies. Place them on a baking sheet lined with parchment paper and bake for approximately 15 minutes or until crisp. Transfer the cookies to a wire rack to cool.
For the icing, mix the confectioners' sugar and lemon juice well. Put the icing in a pastry bag and decorate the cooled cookies with it.

Preparation time: 25 minutes (excluding resting time for the dough)

Anise cookies

generous 1 cup/150 g flour
7 tbsp/100 g chilled butter, cut
into small pieces
1 egg yolk
1 pinch salt
¾ cup/110 g sugar

1 tsp vanilla sugar or
⅛ tsp vanilla extract
1 egg white
⅛ tsp anise powder
⅛ tsp crushed anise seed

Sift the flour onto a work surface and form a hollow in the middle. Place the butter, egg yolk, salt,
2 tbsp/20 g of the sugar and the vanilla sugar (if using extract, add with the egg white) in the hollow.
Quickly knead everything by hand into a smooth dough. Cover it in plastic wrap and refrigerate
overnight.
Preheat the oven to 340°F/170°C. On a work surface dusted with flour, roll out the dough to a
thickness of ca. ⅛ inch/4 mm. Place the cookies on a baking sheet lined with parchment paper.
Beat the egg whites until stiff and gradually add the remaining sugar. Fold in the anise powder and
anise seed. Fill a pastry bag with the egg white mixture and pipe it onto the cookies. Bake for 15 to
20 minutes or until golden brown.

Preparation time: 45 minutes (excluding resting time for the dough)

Jelly cookies

1 ¾ cups/250 g flour
1 ½ tsp baking powder
5 tbsp/70 g sugar
1 egg
1 pinch salt
9 tbsp/125 g chilled butter

½ cup/150 g redcurrant jelly
confectioners' sugar

Sift the flour and baking powder onto a work surface. Form a hollow in the middle and place the sugar, egg and salt in it. Cut the butter into small pieces and place it on the outer edge of the mound, then quickly knead everything by hand into a smooth dough. Cover the dough in plastic wrap and let it rest in the fridge for 1 hour.

Preheat the oven to 340°F/170°C. Divide the dough in half. On a floured work surface, roll out the first half thinly and cut out the cookies. Roll out the second half of the dough, cut out the cookies and use a thimble or other small round object to remove a small circle of dough from the middle of each one.

Put the cookies on a baking sheet lined with parchment paper and bake for 8 to 10 minutes. Let cool. Meanwhile, heat the jelly in a saucepan and brush onto the cookies without holes. Place the cookies with holes on top and sprinkle with confectioners' sugar.

Preparation time: 40 minutes (excluding resting time for the dough)

Chocolate hazelnut cookies

2 ¼ cups/250 g confectioners' sugar
1 ½ cups/120 g ground hazelnuts
1 ⅓ cups/120 g ground almonds
pulp of ½ vanilla bean
1 egg
1 egg yolk

5–6 oz dark chocolate (coating chocolate, if available)
⅛ tsp ground cloves
4 oz/120 g double cream (or highest fat cream available) at room temperature
confectioners' sugar

Mix together the confectioners' sugar, hazelnuts, almonds and vanilla pulp in a bowl. Add the egg and egg yolk and knead everything by hand into a smooth dough. Cover in plastic wrap and chill in the fridge for 30 minutes.

Preheat the oven to 390 °F/200 °C. Dust a work surface with a little confectioners' sugar and roll out the dough to a thickness of ca. ⅕ inch/5 mm. Cut out the cookies and place them on a baking sheet lined with parchment paper, leaving space between them. Bake for approximately 10 minutes. Transfer the cookies to a rack and let cool.

Cut the dark chocolate into small pieces and melt in a double boiler. Sprinkle the ground cloves over the melted chocolate, remove from the double boiler, and fold in the cream until the coating is a uniform color. Cool the mixture until spreadable. Use a spoon to spread a little chocolate coating on half of the cookies, then top with another cookie. Allow to dry and then sprinkle with confectioners' sugar.

Preparation time: 25 minutes (excluding resting time for the dough)

Orange cookies

1 ⅓ cups/300 g butter at room temperature	2–3 drops orange oil or extract
1 ⅓ cups/150 g confectioners' sugar, sifted	2 ¼ cups/300 g flour
3 egg yolks	For the icing:
⅛ tsp vanilla seeds	scant 1 cup/100 g confectioners' sugar, sifted
1 tsp grated orange peel	3 tbsp orange liqueur

Beat the butter and sugar with an electric mixer. Gradually add the egg yolks and beat until mixture is creamy. Stir in the vanilla seeds, orange peel, orange oil and blend the flour into the dough one spoonful at a time. Form the dough into 2 balls, cover in plastic wrap and refrigerate overnight.
Preheat the oven to 340°F/170°C. On a floured work surface, roll out both of the balls of dough and cut out the cookies. Bake for approximately 15 minutes or until the edges of the cookies are just slightly brown. Transfer them to a rack to cool.
For the icing, stir together the confectioners' sugar and orange liqueur until the icing is smooth and thick. Brush onto the cookies.

Preparation time: 35 minutes (excluding resting time for the dough)

Butter cookies

1 ¾ cups/250 g flour
⅓ cup/75 g sugar
1 pinch salt
2 tsp vanilla extract
1 egg
9 tbsp/125 g chilled butter

Place all the ingredients in a bowl and use your hands, preferably not too warm, to quickly knead everything into a firm dough. Cover the dough in plastic wrap and let it rest in the fridge for 2 hours. Preheat the oven to 390°F/200°C. On a floured work surface, roll out the dough to a thickness of ca. ⅕ inch/5 mm. Cut out the cookies and place them on a baking sheet lined with parchment paper. Bake for 10 to 13 minutes or until golden brown. Remove the cookies and transfer to a rack to cool.

Preparation time: 25 minutes (excluding resting time for the dough)

Colorful Christmas cookies

1 ¾ cups/250 g flour
1 cup + 2 tbsp/125 g confectioners' sugar
1 tbsp grated lemon peel
1 egg
⅔ cup/150 g chilled butter

For the icing:
1¾ cups/200 g confectioners' sugar
1 tsp lemon juice
1 tsp rum
1 tsp raspberry syrup
decorative sugar crystals

Place the flour, confectioners' sugar, lemon peel, egg and butter cut into small pieces in a bowl. Using your hands, knead everything into a dough. Cover in plastic wrap and place in the fridge for 2 hours. Preheat the oven to 355 °F/180 °C and line a baking sheet with parchment paper. On a floured surface, roll out the dough to a thickness of about ⅛ inch/4 mm. Cut out the cookies and place them on the baking sheet. Bake for approximately 10 minutes or until golden brown. Transfer the cookies to a rack and let cool thoroughly.
For the icing, mix two-thirds of the confectioners' sugar with the lemon juice and rum. Brush onto the cookies. Make a glaze from the remaining confectioners' sugar and the raspberry syrup. Fill a pastry bag with this mixture and use it to decorate the cookies. Top off with sugar crystals and let the icing dry.

Preparation time: 35 minutes (excluding resting time for the dough)

Pistachio cookies

1 ¾ cups/250 g flour
generous ½ cup/50 g ground almonds
scant 1 cup/75 g ground pistachio nuts
⅓ cup/75 g sugar
2 tsp vanilla sugar or

¼ tsp vanilla extract
⅔ cup/150 g butter
2 egg yolks
1 tsp ground cardamom
1 tbsp confectioners' sugar
2 tbsp ground pistachio nuts
2 tbsp decorating sugar

Combine the flour, ground almonds and pistachios, sugar, vanilla, butter, egg yolks and cardamom and knead by hand to form a smooth dough. Cover it and chill in the fridge for about 2 hours.
Preheat the oven to 355 °F/180 °C. Roll out the dough on a floured work surface. Cut out the cookies and place on a baking sheet lined with parchment paper. Bake for approximately 12 minutes.
Stir the confectioners' sugar and a little water into a not-too-stiff icing. On a flat plate, combine the decorating sugar and ground pistachios. While still warm, brush the cookies with icing, then dredge in the sugar-pistachio mixture.

Preparation time: 35 minutes (excluding resting time for the dough)

Sugar-pearl cookies

7 oz/200 g marzipan paste
2 cups/220 g confectioners' sugar
3 tbsp lemon juice
food coloring
sugar pearls
decorative sugar crystals

Cover a baking sheet with parchment paper and preheat the oven to 390 °F/200 °C.
Knead slightly less than half the confectioners' sugar into the raw marzipan and roll it out thinly
between two sheets of parchment paper. Cut out the cookies and place them on the baking sheet.
Bake for approximately 5 minutes, then transfer to a rack to cool.
For the icing, stir together the remaining confectioners' sugar and lemon juice until smooth.
Tint the icing with food coloring, if desired, and brush it onto the cookies.
Decorate any way you like, either with sugar pearls or decorative sugar crystals.

Preparation time: 20 minutes

Tipsy cookies

3 ¾ cups/500 g flour
1 tsp baking powder
1 cup + 2 tbsp/250 g sugar
1 egg
2 tbsp cocoa powder
2 tsp cinnamon

1 ¼ cups/280 g butter
½ cup red wine
1 ⅓ cups/150 g confectioners' sugar

Sift the flour onto a work surface or into a bowl. Add the baking powder, sugar, egg, cocoa powder, cinnamon, butter and 6 tablespoons of the red wine and quickly knead everything by hand into a smooth dough. Form the dough into a ball, cover it with plastic wrap and let it rest in the fridge for 1 hour.

Preheat the oven to 355 °F/180 °C. On a floured work surface, roll out the dough thinly. Cut out the cookies and place them on a baking sheet lined with parchment paper. Bake the cookies for approximately 10 minutes, then allow to cool. To make the icing, mix the confectioners' sugar and remaining wine until smooth. Fill a pastry bag with the icing and decorate the cookies.

Preparation time: 20 minutes (excluding resting time for the dough)

Colorful apricot cookies

14 tbsp/200 g butter	freshly ground nutmeg
6 tbsp/80 g sugar	2 ¼ cups/300 g flour
1 pinch salt	2–3 tbsp/50 g apricot jam
2 tsp vanilla sugar or	scant 1 cup/100 g confectioners'
¼ tsp vanilla extract	sugar
1 egg yolk	2–3 tbsp lemon juice
4 tbsp Cognac	red food coloring

In a bowl, beat the butter, sugar, salt and vanilla sugar (if using extract, add with the egg yolk) until creamy. Stir in the egg yolk along with the cognac and nutmeg. Quickly mix in the flour. Roll out the dough between two layers of plastic wrap or wax paper to a thickness of ⅛ inch/4 mm. Place the sheets of dough and the cookie cutter in the fridge for 2 hours.

Preheat the oven to 355°F/180°C. Cut out the cookies with the chilled cookie cutter, place them on a baking sheet lined with parchment paper, and bake for approximately 12 minutes or until golden brown.

Take the baking sheet out of the oven. Let the cookies cool slightly on the sheet, then transfer them to a rack to finish cooling. Warm the apricot jam in a small saucepan. Spread it on half of the cookies and place the remaining cookies on top.

Stir together the confectioners' sugar and lemon juice to make an icing. Set aside some of the white icing and add red food coloring to the rest. Spread red icing on the cookies and let dry. Fill a pastry bag with white icing and decorate the cookies with it.

Preparation time: 50 minutes (excluding resting time for the dough)

Slivered almond cookies

generous 1 cup/150 g flour
1 tsp baking powder
7 tbsp/100 g butter
¼ cup/50 g sugar
1 pinch salt
2 tsp vanilla sugar

or ¼ tsp vanilla extract
1 egg
14 oz/400 g bittersweet
chocolate (coating chocolate,
if available)
2¾ cups/300 g slivered almonds

Sift the flour into a bowl. Add the baking powder, butter, sugar, salt, vanilla and egg. Knead by hand to form a smooth dough. Form it into a ball, cover in plastic wrap and let it rest in the fridge for 1 hour.

Preheat the oven to 390 °F/200 °C and cover a baking sheet with parchment paper. On a floured work surface, roll out the dough and cut out the cookies. Place the cookies on the baking sheet and bake for 8 to 10 minutes. Meanwhile, melt the bittersweet chocolate in a double boiler and fold in the slivered almonds.

Take the cookies out of the oven and let them cool briefly. Use two teaspoons to top each cookie with some of the almond mixture. Place on a rack to dry.

Preparation time: 50 minutes (excluding resting time for the dough)

Cinnamon cookies

2 ¼ cups/250 g confectioners'
sugar
3 egg whites
2 ¼ cups/200 g ground whole
almonds
1 tsp ground cinnamon

1 tbsp rum
2 tsp vanilla sugar or ¼ tsp vanilla
extract

Sift the confectioners' sugar. Beat the egg whites until very stiff and gradually add the confectioners'
sugar. Set aside ½ cup of the egg whites to brush on later. Fold the ground almonds, cinnamon, rum
and vanilla into the larger portion of egg whites.
Preheat the oven to 265 °F/130 °C. Sprinkle the work surface generously with confectioners' sugar
and roll out the dough to a thickness of about ⅕ inch/5 mm. Cut out the cookies and place them on
a baking sheet lined with parchment paper. Brush the tops with the reserved egg white and let the
cookies "dry" rather than bake in the oven for 30 to 40 minutes.

Preparation time: 50 minutes (excluding resting time for the dough)

Cookie

Classics

Spiced oatmeal cookies

½ cup/75 g flour
1 ½ tsp baking powder
¼ cup/50 g sugar
1 ¼ cups/175 g fine oatmeal
or rolled oats
¼ cup/50 g finely chopped pitted
prunes

½ tsp cinnamon, ½ tsp ground
ginger, 1 pinch salt
2 ½ tbsp/40 g butter, cut in small
pieces
3 tbsp molasses or treacle
1 egg
confectioners' sugar for dusting

Combine the flour, baking powder, sugar and oats. Stir in the chopped prunes, spices and salt. Using the dough hook attachment of an electric mixer, work in the butter. Warm the molasses so that it becomes more fluid. Let it cool slightly and stir it into the dough along with the egg. Preheat the oven to 355 °F/180 °C and line a baking sheet with parchment paper. Using a teaspoon, place little dollops of dough on the baking sheet, leaving plenty of space between them. Bake the cookies on the second to lowest rack of the oven for approximately 10 minutes. Transfer the cookies to a cookie rack to cool and dust with confectioners' sugar.

Preparation time: 30 minutes

Caramel apple cookies

9 oz/250 g apple
1 ¾ cups/150 g dried apple rings
1 ½ cups/200 g flour
1 cup/150 g oats
1 pinch salt, 1 tsp baking powder
9 tbsp/120 g butter
¾ cup + 2 tbsp/200 g brown cane

sugar (sucanat) or brown sugar
2 tsp vanilla sugar or ¼ tsp vanilla
extract
1 egg, 2 tbsp milk
Scant ⅔ cup/130 g brown cane
sugar (sucanat) or brown sugar
5 tbsp cream, 3 tbsp maple syrup

Finely dice the fresh and dried apples. Combine the flour, oats, salt and baking powder in a small bowl. Beat the butter in a larger mixing bowl, then add the brown sugar and vanilla and beat well. Mix in the egg and milk. Beat the batter until frothy. Add the flour mixture and diced apples to the mixing bowl. Knead with the dough hook of a hand mixer to combine, then knead everything by hand into a smooth dough. Roll the dough into logs with a diameter of ca. ¾ inch/2 cm. Cover them with plastic wrap and let rest in the fridge for 30 minutes.

Preheat the oven to 355 °F/180 °C and line a baking sheet with parchment paper. Cut the dough into slices ca. ⅓ inch/1 cm thick. Place them on the baking sheet and press lightly to flatten them. Bake on the middle rack of the oven for approximately 10 minutes.

For the icing, carefully melt the brown sugar in a small pan over low heat. Add the cream and maple syrup. Bring to a boil, stirring continuously. Remove from the heat and continue stirring so that the caramel melts completely.

Lets the cookies cool slightly, then cover them with warm caramel icing.

Preparation time: 45 minutes (excluding resting time for the dough)

Peanut butter cookies

⅔ cup/150 g butter	1 tsp baking powder
⅔ cup/150 g sugar	1 ¾ cups/200 g walnuts
2 tsp vanilla sugar or	⅔ cup/100 g roasted peanuts
¼ tsp vanilla extract	2 oz/50 g chocolate, grated
½ cup/125 g peanut butter, 1 egg	2 tbsp confectioners' sugar
2 ¼ cups/300 g flour	1 tbsp cocoa powder

Beat the butter, sugar and vanilla sugar (if using extract, add with the egg) until light and fluffy. Thoroughly mix in the peanut butter and egg. Combine the flour and baking powder and rapidly stir them in as well. Chop the walnuts and peanuts and fold them into the dough with the grated chocolate. Form the dough into finger-width rolls.

Preheat the oven to 355 °F/180 °C and line a baking sheet with parchment paper. Cut the dough rolls into walnut-sized portions, form into balls, and place them on the baking sheet, leaving some space between them. Gently press each cookie flat with a fork and bake on the middle rack of the oven for about 12 minutes.

Transfer the cookies to a rack to cool and dust with a mixture of confectioners' sugar and cocoa powder.

Preparation time: 45 minutes

Cranberry cookies

⅔ cup/150 g butter
1 cup/200 g brown sugar
1 egg
1 ½ cups/200 g flour
1 ½ tsp baking powder
1 pinch salt

⅔ cup/75 g walnuts
generous ¾ cup/100 g dried
cranberries
2 oz/50 g bittersweet chocolate
(coating chocolate, if available)

Beat the butter and sugar thoroughly. Stir in the egg and beat until creamy and even. Combine the flour and baking powder, then stir in rapidly along with the salt. Chop the walnuts and fold them and the cranberries into the dough.

Preheat the oven to 355 °F/180 °C. Cover two baking sheets with parchment paper. Using a teaspoon, place small dollops of cookie dough on the sheets, leaving plenty of space in between. Bake the cookies on the middle rack of the oven for approximately 12 minutes. Transfer the cookies to a rack and let cool.

Melt the bittersweet chocolate in a double boiler. Use a piece of parchment paper to form a small pastry cone with a narrow opening. Squeeze the chocolate onto the fully cooled cookies, creating a striped pattern.

Preparation time: 30 minutes

Oatmeal coconut dollars

7 tbsp/100 g butter
7 tbsp/100 g demerara sugar
¼ cup/50 g white sugar
2 tsp vanilla sugar or
¼ tsp vanilla extract
1 egg, 1 tsp baking powder

1 pinch salt
¾ cup + 2 tbsp/125 g flour
½ cup/70 g fine oatmeal
or rolled oats
⅔ cup/60 g flaked coconut +
7 tbsp/40 g for decoration

Thoroughly beat the butter with the demerara, white and vanilla sugar (if using extract, add with the egg). Add the egg and stir in well. Combine the baking powder, salt, flour, oats and ⅔ cup/ 60 g flaked coconut, then stir the mixture into the batter.

Preheat the oven to 355 °F/180 °C and line a baking sheet with parchment paper. Using a teaspoon, place small mounds of dough on the baking sheet, leaving plenty of space between them. Sprinkle the remaining coconut on the cookies.

Bake the cookies on the middle rack of the oven for about 10 minutes. Transfer to a rack to cool.

Preparation time: 30 minutes

Christmas fruit cookies

7 tbsp/100 g butter
¾ cup + 2 tbsp/125 g sugar
generous ¾ cup/200 g cream
2 oz/50 g red and green candied
cherries

6 tbsp/50 g dried currants
or raisins
2¾ cups/250 g ground almonds
⅔ cup/100 g flour
⅓ cup/50 g whole almonds

Melt the butter in a pan over low heat, then add the sugar
and cream and briefly bring to a boil. Pour the mixture into a
mixing bowl. Chop the candied cherries and add them to the
bowl along with the currants, ground almonds and flour. Stir
everything thoroughly with a spoon. Blanch the whole almonds,
rinse in cold water and remove the skins.
Preheat the oven to 355°F/180°C. Use a teaspoon to place
small mounds of dough on a baking sheet lined with parchment
paper, leaving plenty of space between them. Decorate each
cookie with an almond half. Bake the cookies on the second to
lowest rack of the oven for approximately 10 minutes.

Preparation time: 30 minutes

Ginger cream sandwich cookies

3⅔ cups/360 g flour
6 tbsp/50 g cornstarch or rice flour
⅔ cup/150 g demerara sugar
2 tsp vanilla sugar or
¼ tsp vanilla extract
1 cup + 2 tbsp/250 g butter

For the ginger cream:
13 tbsp/180 g butter
generous ¾ cup/90 g
confectioners' sugar
3 tbsp finely chopped candied
ginger

Sift the flour and cornstarch or rice flour onto a work surface.
Sprinkle the demerara sugar and vanilla on top, and
distribute the butter, cut into small pieces, around the edges.
Knead by hand into a smooth dough. Form the dough into rolls
ca. ¾ inch/2 cm in diameter, cover them in plastic wrap and let
them chill in the fridge for about 30 minutes.
Preheat the oven to 355°F/180°C. Slice the rolls into disks ca.
⅓ inch/1 cm thick and place them on a baking sheet lined with
parchment paper. Use a fork to make a lattice pattern on top of
each cookie. Bake the cookies on the middle rack of the oven
for approximately 12 minutes or until golden brown.
For the ginger cream filling, whip the butter and confectioners'
sugar until creamy with an electric mixer and wire whip
attachment. Stir in the ginger. Spread ginger cream on half of
the cooled cookies, and place another cookie on top to make
sandwiches.

Preparation time: 45 minutes (excluding resting time for the dough)

Whiskey fruit cookies

11 oz/300 g red and green candied cherries	(sucanat) or brown sugar
11 oz/300 g candied pineapple	2 eggs
3 cups/300 g pecan halves	1 ¼ cups/180 g flour
2 cups/300 g chopped dried dates	1 ½ tsp baking soda
4 tbsp/50 g butter	½ tsp grated nutmeg
7 tbsp/100 g brown cane sugar	1 ½ tbsp milk
	½ cup/120 ml whiskey

Finely chop the candied cherries, candied pineapple and pecans. Beat the butter and sugar in a mixing bowl until light and fluffy. Add the eggs and stir in well. Combine the flour, baking soda and nutmeg and add to the butter mixture, stirring just to combine. Mix in the candied fruits, pecans, dates, milk and whiskey.

Preheat the oven to 355 °F/180 °C and line a baking sheet with parchment paper. Using a teaspoon, place small mounds of dough on the baking sheet, leaving plenty of space between them. Bake the cookies on the middle rack of the oven for approximately 15 minutes. Transfer to a rack to cool.

Preparation time: 45 minutes

Chocolate mounds

7 oz/200 g bittersweet chocolate
7 oz/200 g milk chocolate
4 cups/120 g corn flakes
generous ½ cup/50 g flaked
coconut

Chop the chocolate into coarse bits and melt in a double boiler, stirring constantly. Allow the melted chocolate to cool slightly and stir well again before folding in the corn flakes with a rubber spatula. Line a baking sheet with parchment paper and place small mounds of the mixture on it. Each mound should be ca. ¾ inch/2 cm in diameter. Since the mixture is rather crumbly, you may need to reshape the cookies with your fingers.

Lightly brown the flaked coconut in a non-stick frying pan and sprinkle it over the chocolate mounds. Allow 1 ½ hours for the chocolate to set before eating.

Preparation time: 30 minutes (excluding time for chocolate to set)

Chocolate caramel cookies

14 tbsp/200 g butter
6 tbsp/80 g sugar
2 tsp vanilla sugar or
¼ tsp vanilla extract
pulp of 1 vanilla bean
1 egg
2 ¼ cups/300 g flour

1 pinch salt, 2 tbsp milk
2 tbsp chocolate liqueur
3–4 oz/100 g soft caramels
(ca. 10 pieces)
7 tbsp/50 g slivered almonds
3–4 oz/100 g bittersweet
chocolate chips

Beat the butter, sugar, vanilla sugar or extract and vanilla pulp until creamy. Add the egg and blend in thoroughly. Combine the flour and salt. Add them to the butter mixture with the milk and chocolate liqueur.

Finely dice the caramel candy and chop the almonds. Fold the caramel, almonds and half the chocolate drops into the dough.

Preheat the oven to 355 °F/180 °C and line a baking sheet with parchment paper. Using a teaspoon, place small mounds of dough on the baking sheet, leaving some space between them. Distribute the remaining chocolate chips on top of the cookies. Bake them on the second lowest oven rack for about 12 minutes, then transfer to a rack to cool.

Preparation time: 45 minutes

Index